THE
ONE-MINUTE
GRATITUDE
JOURNAL

for

JOURNAL TO INCREASE GRATITUDE, MINDFULNESS AND HAPPINESS

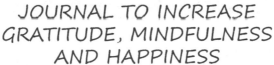

This Journal belongs to:

_____

ISBN: 978-1-952358-26-5

Date: _____

ABOUT ME

My name is

_____

I am _____ years old

My family

I like to...

My big dreams...

Date: __/__/____   S M T W T F S

I am thankful for:

⭐ ❶ _____

⭐ ❷ _____

⭐ ❸ _____

Today I learned about...

Something I did today that was amazing...

How would you rate today? ☆ ☆ ☆ ☆ ☆

What made you happy today? Draw or write.

Date: __/__/____   S M T W T F S

I am thankful for:

① _____

② _____

③ _____

Today I learned about...

Something I did today that was kind...

I feel 😟 😖 🙁 😮 😐 🙂 😄

What made you happy today? Draw or write.

Date: __/__/____   S M T W T F S

I am thankful for:

⭐ ❶ _____

⭐ ❷ _____

⭐ ❸ _____

Today I learned about...

Something I did today that was amazing...

How would you rate today? ☆ ☆ ☆ ☆ ☆

What made you happy today? Draw or write.

Date: ___/___/_____   S M T W T F S

I am thankful for:

⭐ **1** _____

⭐ **2** _____

⭐ **3** _____

Today I learned about...

Something I did today that was kind...

I feel

What made you happy today? Draw or write.

Date: __/__/____   S M T W T F S

I am thankful for:

① _____

② _____

③ _____

Today I learned about...

Something I did today that was amazing...

How would you rate today? ☆ ☆ ☆ ☆ ☆

What made you happy today? Draw or write.

Date: __/__/____   S M T W T F S

I am thankful for:

⭐❶ _____

⭐❷ _____

⭐❸ _____

Today I learned about...

Something I did today that was kind...

I feel 😟 😖 🙁 😮 😐 🙂 😄

What made you happy today? Draw or write.

GRATITUDE JAR

Fill this jar with everything you are grateful for!

Date: _____

Date: __/__/____   S M T W T F S

I am thankful for:

⭐❶ _____

⭐❷ _____

⭐❸ _____

Today I learned about...

Something I did today that was kind...

I feel 😟 😑 🙁 😮 😐 🙂 😄

What made you happy today? Draw or write.

Date: __/__/____   S M T W T F S

I am thankful for:

① _____

② _____

③ _____

Today I learned about...

Something I did today that was amazing...

How would you rate today? ☆ ☆ ☆ ☆ ☆

What made you happy today? Draw or write.

Date: __/__/____   S M T W T F S

I am thankful for:

⭐ ❶ _____

⭐ ❷ _____

⭐ ❸ _____

Today I learned about...

Something I did today that was kind...

I feel 😟 😖 🙁 😳 😐 🙂 😄

What made you happy today? Draw or write.

Date: __/__/____   S M T W T F S

I am thankful for:

❶ _____

❷ _____

❸ _____

Today I learned about...

Something I did today that was amazing...

How would you rate today? ☆☆☆☆☆

What made you happy today? Draw or write.

Date: ___/___/_____   S   M   T   W   T   F   S

I am thankful for:

⭐ ❶ _____

⭐ ❷ _____

⭐ ❸ _____

Today I learned about...

Something I did today that was kind...

I feel 😟 😣 🙁 😮 😐 🙂 😃

What made you happy today? Draw or write.

Date: __/__/___   S M T W T F S

I am thankful for:

① _____

② _____

③ _____

Today I learned about...

Something I did today that was amazing...

How would you rate today? ☆ ☆ ☆ ☆ ☆

What made you happy today? Draw or write.

Date: _____

PEOPLE I LOVE

ME

_____
Name

Date: __/__/____   S M T W T F S

I am thankful for:

⭐❶ _____

⭐❷ _____

⭐❸ _____

Today I learned about...

Something I did today that was amazing...

How would you rate today? ☆ ☆ ☆ ☆ ☆

What made you happy today? Draw or write.

Date: __/__/____   S M T W T F S

I am thankful for:

⭐❶ _____

⭐❷ _____

⭐❸ _____

Today I learned about...

Something I did today that was kind...

I feel 😖 😣 🙁 😮 😐 🙂 😄

What made you happy today? Draw or write.

Date: __/__/____   S M T W T F S

I am thankful for:

⭐ ❶ _____

⭐ ❷ _____

⭐ ❸ _____

Today I learned about...

Something I did today that was amazing...

How would you rate today? ☆ ☆ ☆ ☆ ☆

What made you happy today? Draw or write.

Date: __/__/____   S M T W T F S

I am thankful for:

⭐ ❶ _____

⭐ ❷ _____

⭐ ❸ _____

Today I learned about...

Something I did today that was kind...

I feel 😵 😑 🙁 😮 😐 🙂 😄

What made you happy today? Draw or write.

Date: __/__/____   S M T W T F S

I am thankful for:

⭐ **❶** _____

⭐ **❷** _____

⭐ **❸** _____

Today I learned about...

Something I did today that was amazing...

How would you rate today? ☆ ☆ ☆ ☆ ☆

What made you happy today? Draw or write.

Date: __/__/____   S M T W T F S

I am thankful for:

① _____

② _____

③ _____

Today I learned about...

Something I did today that was kind...

I feel 😖 😣 😟 😮 😐 🙂 😃

What made you happy today? Draw or write.

Find something blue. Draw or write about it.

Date: _____

Date: __/__/____   S   M   T   W   T   F   S

I am thankful for:

⭐❶ _____

⭐❷ _____

⭐❸ _____

Today I learned about...

Something I did today that was kind...

I feel 😟 😣 🙁 😮 😐 🙂 😃

What made you happy today? Draw or write.

Date: __/__/____   S M T W T F S

I am thankful for:

⭐ **1** _____

⭐ **2** _____

⭐ **3** _____

Today I learned about...

Something I did today that was amazing...

How would you rate today? ☆ ☆ ☆ ☆ ☆

What made you happy today? Draw or write.

Date: __/__/____   S M T W T F S

I am thankful for:

⭐ ❶ _____

⭐ ❷ _____

⭐ ❸ _____

Today I learned about...

Something I did today that was kind...

I feel 😵 😑 🙁 😲 😐 🙂 😃

What made you happy today? Draw or write.

Date: __/__/____   S M T W T F S

I am thankful for:

⭐ **1** _____

⭐ **2** _____

⭐ **3** _____

Today I learned about...

Something I did today that was amazing...

How would you rate today? ☆ ☆ ☆ ☆ ☆

What made you happy today? Draw or write.

Date: __/__/____   S M T W T F S

I am thankful for:

⭐ ❶ _____

⭐ ❷ _____

⭐ ❸ _____

Today I learned about...

Something I did today that was kind...

I feel 😖 😐 😟 😯 😑 🙂 😃

What made you happy today? Draw or write.

Date: __/__/____   S M T W T F S

I am thankful for:

⭐ ❶ _____

⭐ ❷ _____

⭐ ❸ _____

Today I learned about...

Something I did today that was amazing...

How would you rate today? ☆ ☆ ☆ ☆ ☆

What made you happy today? Draw or write.

Date: _____

5 THINGS THAT MAKE ME LAUGH

1. _____

2. _____

3. _____

4. _____

5. _____

Date: __/__/____   S M T W T F S

I am thankful for:

❶ _____

❷ _____

❸ _____

Today I learned about...

Something I did today that was amazing...

How would you rate today? ☆☆☆☆☆

What made you happy today? Draw or write.

Date: __/__/____   S M T W T F S

I am thankful for:

⭐❶ _____

⭐❷ _____

⭐❸ _____

Today I learned about...

Something I did today that was kind...

I feel 😟 😣 😦 😮 😐 🙂 😃

What made you happy today? Draw or write.

Date: __/__/____   S M T W T F S

I am thankful for:

⭐ **❶** _____

⭐ **❷** _____

⭐ **❸** _____

Today I learned about...

Something I did today that was amazing...

How would you rate today? ☆ ☆ ☆ ☆ ☆

What made you happy today? Draw or write.

Date: __/__/____   S M T W T F S

I am thankful for:

❶ _____

❷ _____

❸ _____

Today I learned about...

Something I did today that was kind...

I feel

What made you happy today? Draw or write.

Date: __/__/____   S M T W T F S

I am thankful for:

⭐ ❶ _____

⭐ ❷ _____

⭐ ❸ _____

Today I learned about...

Something I did today that was amazing...

How would you rate today? ☆ ☆ ☆ ☆ ☆

What made you happy today? Draw or write.

Date: __/__/____   S M T W T F S

I am thankful for:

⭐ ❶ _____

⭐ ❷ _____

⭐ ❸ _____

Today I learned about...

Something I did today that was kind...

I feel 😟 😖 🙁 😳 😐 🙂 😃

What made you happy today? Draw or write.

Date: _____

Something I'm afraid of.

_____

Something I'm excited about.

_____

Something I like to listen to.

_____

Something I like to eat.

_____

Something I like to touch.

_____

Date: __/__/____   S M T W T F S

I am thankful for:

⭐❶ _____

⭐❷ _____

⭐❸ _____

Today I learned about...

Something I did today that was kind...

I feel 😖 😣 🙁 😮 😐 🙂 😀

What made you happy today? Draw or write.

Date: __/__/____   S M T W T F S

I am thankful for:

⭐ ❶ _____

⭐ ❷ _____

⭐ ❸ _____

Today I learned about...

Something I did today that was amazing...

How would you rate today? ☆ ☆ ☆ ☆ ☆

What made you happy today? Draw or write.

Date: __/__/____   S   M   T   W   T   F   S

I am thankful for:

① _____

② _____

③ _____

Today I learned about...

Something I did today that was kind...

I feel

What made you happy today? Draw or write.

Date: __/__/____   S M T W T F S

I am thankful for:

⭐❶ _____

⭐❷ _____

⭐❸ _____

Today I learned about...

Something I did today that was amazing...

How would you rate today? ☆ ☆ ☆ ☆ ☆

What made you happy today? Draw or write.

Date: __/__/____   S M T W T F S

I am thankful for:

⭐① _____

⭐② _____

⭐③ _____

Today I learned about...

Something I did today that was kind...

I feel 😟 😖 🙁 😯 😐 🙂 😄

What made you happy today? Draw or write.

Date: __/__/____   S   M   T   W   T   F   S

I am thankful for:

⭐ ❶ _____

⭐ ❷ _____

⭐ ❸ _____

Today I learned about...

Something I did today that was amazing...

How would you rate today? ☆ ☆ ☆ ☆ ☆

What made you happy today? Draw or write.

Date: _____

10 THINGS I LOVE

1. _____

2. _____

3. _____

4. _____

5. _____

6. _____

7. _____

8. _____

9. _____

10. _____

Date: __/__/____   S M T W T F S

I am thankful for:

⭐ ❶ _____

⭐ ❷ _____

⭐ ❸ _____

Today I learned about...

Something I did today that was amazing...

How would you rate today? ☆ ☆ ☆ ☆ ☆

What made you happy today? Draw or write.

Date: __/__/____   S   M   T   W   T   F   S

I am thankful for:

⭐❶ _____

⭐❷ _____

⭐❸ _____

Today I learned about...

Something I did today that was kind...

I feel

What made you happy today? Draw or write.

Date: __/__/____   S M T W T F S

I am thankful for:

1. _____

2. _____

3. _____

Today I learned about...

Something I did today that was amazing...

How would you rate today? ☆ ☆ ☆ ☆ ☆

What made you happy today? Draw or write.

Date: __/__/____   S M T W T F S

I am thankful for:

⭐❶ _____

⭐❷ _____

⭐❸ _____

Today I learned about...

Something I did today that was kind...

I feel 😣 😖 😟 😮 😐 🙂 😄

What made you happy today? Draw or write.

Date: __/__/____   S   M   T   W   T   F   S

I am thankful for:

① _____

② _____

③ _____

Today I learned about...

Something I did today that was amazing...

How would you rate today? ☆ ☆ ☆ ☆ ☆

What made you happy today? Draw or write.

Date: __/__/____   S M T W T F S

I am thankful for:

⭐❶ _____

⭐❷ _____

⭐❸ _____

Today I learned about...

Something I did today that was kind...

I feel 😖 😵 🙁 😮 😐 🙂 😀

What made you happy today? Draw or write.

ACTIVITY

(complete all the activities)

Dance for 1 minute!	Share something with a friend!	Send a thank you note to someone!
Read a poem out loud!	Tell a joke!	Listen to someone for 1 minute!
Draw something and give it to someone!	Sing someone a song for 1 minute!	Thank someone for no reason!

Date completed: _____

Date: __/__/___   S M T W T F S

I am thankful for:

❶ _____

❷ _____

❸ _____

Today I learned about...

Something I did today that was kind...

I feel

What made you happy today? Draw or write.

Date: __/__/____   S M T W T F S

I am thankful for:

⭐❶ _____

⭐❷ _____

⭐❸ _____

Today I learned about...

Something I did today that was amazing...

How would you rate today? ☆ ☆ ☆ ☆ ☆

What made you happy today? Draw or write.

Date: __/__/____   S M T W T F S

I am thankful for:

⭐① _____

⭐② _____

⭐③ _____

Today I learned about...

Something I did today that was kind...

I feel 😖 😵 😟 😮 😐 🙂 😄

What made you happy today? Draw or write.

Date: __/__/____   S   M   T   W   T   F   S

I am thankful for:

⭐ ❶ _____

⭐ ❷ _____

⭐ ❸ _____

Today I learned about...

Something I did today that was amazing...

How would you rate today? ☆ ☆ ☆ ☆ ☆

What made you happy today? Draw or write.

Date: __/__/____   S M T W T F S

I am thankful for:

⭐❶ _____

⭐❷ _____

⭐❸ _____

Today I learned about...

Something I did today that was kind...

I feel 😟 😐 🙁 😮 😐 🙂 😃

What made you happy today? Draw or write.

Date: __/__/____   S M T W T F S

I am thankful for:

⭐ ❶ _____
⭐ ❷ _____
⭐ ❸ _____

Today I learned about...

Something I did today that was amazing...

How would you rate today? ☆ ☆ ☆ ☆ ☆

What made you happy today? Draw or write.

Date: _____

TOP 10 PLACES I WANT TO VISIT

1. _____

2. _____

3. _____

4. _____

5. _____

6. _____

7. _____

8. _____

9. _____

10. _____

Date: __/__/____   S M T W T F S

I am thankful for:

⭐❶ _____

⭐❷ _____

⭐❸ _____

Today I learned about...

Something I did today that was amazing...

How would you rate today? ☆☆☆☆☆

What made you happy today? Draw or write.

Date: __/__/____   S M T W T F S

I am thankful for:

⭐❶ _____

⭐❷ _____

⭐❸ _____

Today I learned about...

Something I did today that was kind...

I feel 😟 😖 😞 😮 😐 🙂 😄

What made you happy today? Draw or write.

Date: __/__/____   S M T W T F S

I am thankful for:

① _____

② _____

③ _____

Today I learned about...

Something I did today that was amazing...

How would you rate today? ☆ ☆ ☆ ☆ ☆

What made you happy today? Draw or write.

Date: __/__/____   S M T W T F S

I am thankful for:

⭐❶ _____

⭐❷ _____

⭐❸ _____

Today I learned about...

Something I did today that was kind...

I feel 😵 😣 🙁 😮 😐 🙂 😃

What made you happy today? Draw or write.

Date: __/__/____   S M T W T F S

I am thankful for:

⭐ ❶ _____

⭐ ❷ _____

⭐ ❸ _____

Today I learned about...

Something I did today that was amazing...

How would you rate today? ☆ ☆ ☆ ☆ ☆

What made you happy today? Draw or write.

Date: __/__/____   S M T W T F S

I am thankful for:

⭐ ❶ _____

⭐ ❷ _____

⭐ ❸ _____

Today I learned about...

Something I did today that was kind...

I feel

What made you happy today? Draw or write.

Date:_____   Dreaming of:

I believe:

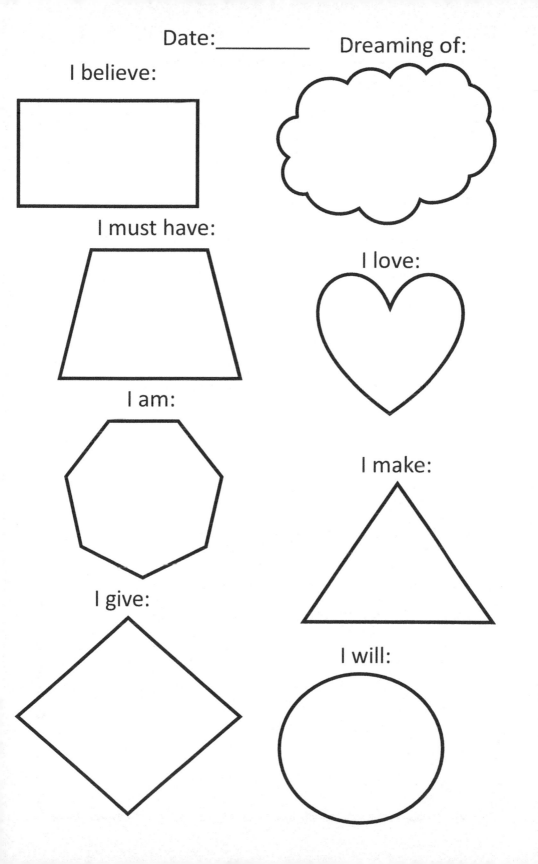

I must have:

I love:

I am:

I make:

I give:

I will:

Date: __ / __ / ____   S M T W T F S

I am thankful for:

⭐❶ _____

⭐❷ _____

⭐❸ _____

Today I learned about...

Something I did today that was kind...

I feel 😟 😖 🙁 😯 😐 🙂 😃

What made you happy today? Draw or write.

Date: ___/___/_____   S M T W T F S

I am thankful for:

⭐ **1** _____

⭐ **2** _____

⭐ **3** _____

Today I learned about...

Something I did today that was amazing...

How would you rate today? ☆ ☆ ☆ ☆ ☆

What made you happy today? Draw or write.

Date: ___/___/_____   S M T W T F S

I am thankful for:

⭐❶ _____

⭐❷ _____

⭐❸ _____

Today I learned about...

Something I did today that was kind...

I feel 😖 😣 🙁 😯 😐 🙂 😀

What made you happy today? Draw or write.

Date: __/__/____   S M T W T F S

I am thankful for:

⭐ ❶ _____

⭐ ❷ _____

⭐ ❸ _____

Today I learned about...

Something I did today that was amazing...

How would you rate today? ☆ ☆ ☆ ☆ ☆

What made you happy today? Draw or write.

Date: __/__/____   S   M   T   W   T   F   S

I am thankful for:

❶ _____

❷ _____

❸ _____

Today I learned about...

Something I did today that was kind...

I feel

What made you happy today? Draw or write.

Date: __/__/____   S M T W T F S

I am thankful for:

⭐❶ _____

⭐❷ _____

⭐❸ _____

Today I learned about...

Something I did today that was amazing...

How would you rate today? ☆☆☆☆☆

What made you happy today? Draw or write.

F	H	A	P	P	Y	C	Q	Z	T
R	D	S	K	P	T	R	U	S	T
I	B	E	Y	M	L	E	S	H	A
E	R	R	Y	D	L	A	U	G	H
N	A	V	U	I	O	T	Y	P	W
D	V	I	C	U	R	I	O	U	S
S	E	C	D	A	K	V	C	D	L
H	R	E	R	F	L	I	J	H	O
I	C	H	E	E	R	T	O	P	V
P	R	B	Q	R	T	Y	Y	I	E

CURIOUS   LAUGH
CHEER   TRUST
HAPPY   FRIENDSHIP
LOVE   CREATIVITY
PLAY   SERVICE
JOY   BRAVE

Date: __/__/____   S M T W T F S

I am thankful for:

❶ _____

❷ _____

❸ _____

Today I learned about...

Something I did today that was amazing...

How would you rate today? ☆☆☆☆☆

What made you happy today? Draw or write.

Date: __/__/____   S M T W T F S

I am thankful for:

⭐ ❶ _____

⭐ ❷ _____

⭐ ❸ _____

Today I learned about...

Something I did today that was kind...

I feel 😖 😣 🙁 😮 😐 🙂 😃

What made you happy today? Draw or write.

Date: __/__/____   S M T W T F S

I am thankful for:

⭐ ❶ _____

⭐ ❷ _____

⭐ ❸ _____

Today I learned about...

Something I did today that was amazing...

How would you rate today? ☆ ☆ ☆ ☆ ☆

What made you happy today? Draw or write.

Date: ___/___/_____   S M T W T F S

I am thankful for:

① _____

② _____

③ _____

Today I learned about...

Something I did today that was kind...

I feel

What made you happy today? Draw or write.

Date: __/__/____   S M T W T F S

I am thankful for:

❶ _____

❷ _____

❸ _____

Today I learned about...

Something I did today that was amazing...

How would you rate today? ☆ ☆ ☆ ☆ ☆

What made you happy today? Draw or write.

Date: __/__/____   S M T W T F S

I am thankful for:

① _____

② _____

③ _____

Today I learned about...

Something I did today that was kind...

I feel 😟 😣 🙁 😮 😐 🙂 😀

What made you happy today? Draw or write.

Mindfulness activity

What are 2 things you can see?

_____

_____

What are 2 things you can touch?

_____

_____

What are 2 things you can hear?

_____

_____

What is 1 thing you can smell?

_____

What is 1 thing you can taste?

_____

Date: __/__/____   S M T W T F S

I am thankful for:

⭐ ❶ _____

⭐ ❷ _____

⭐ ❸ _____

Today I learned about...

Something I did today that was kind...

I feel 😵 😑 🙁 😮 😐 🙂 😀

What made you happy today? Draw or write.

Date: ___/___/_____   S M T W T F S

I am thankful for:

⭐❶ _____

⭐❷ _____

⭐❸ _____

Today I learned about...

Something I did today that was amazing...

How would you rate today? ☆ ☆ ☆ ☆ ☆

What made you happy today? Draw or write.

Date: __/__/____   S M T W T F S

I am thankful for:

① _____

② _____

③ _____

Today I learned about...

Something I did today that was kind...

I feel 😟 😣 🙁 😮 😐 🙂 😀

What made you happy today? Draw or write.

Date: __ / __ / ____   S M T W T F S

I am thankful for:

⭐ ❶ _____

⭐ ❷ _____

⭐ ❸ _____

Today I learned about...

Something I did today that was amazing...

How would you rate today? ☆ ☆ ☆ ☆ ☆

What made you happy today? Draw or write.

Date: __/__/____   S M T W T F S

I am thankful for:

⭐❶ _____

⭐❷ _____

⭐❸ _____

Today I learned about...

Something I did today that was kind...

I feel 😖 😣 🙁 😮 😐 🙂 😃

What made you happy today? Draw or write.

Date: __/__/____   S M T W T F S

I am thankful for:

★ ❶ _____

★ ❷ _____

★ ❸ _____

Today I learned about...

Something I did today that was amazing...

How would you rate today? ☆ ☆ ☆ ☆ ☆

What made you happy today? Draw or write.

Date: _____

Find a unique stone. Draw and write about it.

Date: __/__/____   S M T W T F S

I am thankful for:

⭐ **1** _____

⭐ **2** _____

⭐ **3** _____

Today I learned about...

Something I did today that was amazing...

How would you rate today? ☆ ☆ ☆ ☆ ☆

What made you happy today? Draw or write.

Date: __/__/____   S M T W T F S

I am thankful for:

① _____

② _____

③ _____

Today I learned about...

Something I did today that was kind...

I feel 😟 😣 🙁 😮 😐 🙂 😃

What made you happy today? Draw or write.

Date: __/__/____   S M T W T F S

I am thankful for:

⭐ ❶ _____

⭐ ❷ _____

⭐ ❸ _____

Today I learned about...

Something I did today that was amazing...

How would you rate today? ☆ ☆ ☆ ☆ ☆

What made you happy today? Draw or write.

Date: __/__/____   S M T W T F S

I am thankful for:

⭐❶ _____

⭐❷ _____

⭐❸ _____

Today I learned about...

Something I did today that was kind...

I feel 😟 😵 🙁 😮 😐 🙂 😃

What made you happy today? Draw or write.

Date: __/__/____   S M T W T F S

I am thankful for:

⭐❶ _____

⭐❷ _____

⭐❸ _____

Today I learned about...

Something I did today that was amazing...

How would you rate today? ☆☆☆☆☆

What made you happy today? Draw or write.

Date: __/__/____   S M T W T F S

I am thankful for:

⭐ ❶ _____

⭐ ❷ _____

⭐ ❸ _____

Today I learned about...

Something I did today that was kind...

I feel 😟 😣 🙁 😮 😐 🙂 😃

What made you happy today? Draw or write.

MINDFULNESS WORD SEARCH

A	C	R	T	F	O	C	U	S	T
Z	P	Y	O	Q	T	H	W	T	O
Q	H	P	I	O	P	E	M	S	U
A	W	A	R	E	U	A	E	M	C
B	T	M	H	E	T	R	D	E	H
T	A	S	T	E	C	S	I	L	F
S	E	E	S	J	L	I	T	L	E
Y	R	Q	K	Z	M	U	A	R	E
L	I	S	T	E	N	R	T	T	L
B	R	E	A	T	H	E	E	U	E

FOCUS   AWARE
APPRECIATE   LISTEN
MEDITATE   TOUCH
HEAR   SEE
BREATHE   TASTE
SMELL   FEEL

Date: __/__/____   S M T W T F S

I am thankful for:

1 _____

2 _____

3 _____

Today I learned about...

Something I did today that was kind...

I feel 😖 😣 🙁 😮 😐 🙂 😄

What made you happy today? Draw or write.

Date: __/__/____   S M T W T F S

I am thankful for:

⭐❶ _____

⭐❷ _____

⭐❸ _____

Today I learned about...

Something I did today that was amazing...

How would you rate today? ☆ ☆ ☆ ☆ ☆

What made you happy today? Draw or write.

Date: __/__/____   S M T W T F S

I am thankful for:

⭐❶ _____

⭐❷ _____

⭐❸ _____

Today I learned about...

Something I did today that was kind...

I feel 😟 😣 🙁 😮 😐 🙂 😀

What made you happy today? Draw or write.

Date: __/__/____   S M T W T F S

I am thankful for:

① _____

② _____

③ _____

Today I learned about...

Something I did today that was amazing...

How would you rate today? ☆ ☆ ☆ ☆ ☆

What made you happy today? Draw or write.

Date: __/__/____   S M T W T F S

I am thankful for:

⭐❶ _____

⭐❷ _____

⭐❸ _____

Today I learned about...

Something I did today that was kind...

I feel 😵 😣 🙁 😮 😐 🙂 😄

What made you happy today? Draw or write.

Date: __ / __ / ____   S M T W T F S

I am thankful for:

⭐❶ _____

⭐❷ _____

⭐❸ _____

Today I learned about...

Something I did today that was amazing...

How would you rate today? ☆ ☆ ☆ ☆ ☆

What made you happy today? Draw or write.

Find something purple. Draw or write about it.

Date: _____

Date: __/__/____   S M T W T F S

I am thankful for:

⭐ ❶ _____

⭐ ❷ _____

⭐ ❸ _____

Today I learned about...

Something I did today that was amazing...

How would you rate today? ☆ ☆ ☆ ☆ ☆

What made you happy today? Draw or write.

Date: __/__/____   S M T W T F S

I am thankful for:

⭐❶ _____

⭐❷ _____

⭐❸ _____

Today I learned about...

Something I did today that was kind...

I feel 😟 😣 🙁 😮 😐 🙂 😀

What made you happy today? Draw or write.

Date: __/__/____   S M T W T F S

I am thankful for:

⭐ ❶ _____

⭐ ❷ _____

⭐ ❸ _____

Today I learned about...

Something I did today that was amazing...

How would you rate today? ☆ ☆ ☆ ☆ ☆

What made you happy today? Draw or write.

Date: __ / __ / ____   S   M   T   W   T   F   S

I am thankful for:

1. _____
2. _____
3. _____

Today I learned about...

Something I did today that was kind...

I feel 🙂 😐 🙁 😮 😑 🙂 😀

What made you happy today? Draw or write.

Date: __/__/____   S M T W T F S

I am thankful for:

⭐❶ _____

⭐❷ _____

⭐❸ _____

Today I learned about...

Something I did today that was amazing...

How would you rate today? ☆☆☆☆☆

What made you happy today? Draw or write.

Date: __/__/____   S M T W T F S

I am thankful for:

⭐ ① _____

⭐ ② _____

⭐ ③ _____

Today I learned about...

Something I did today that was kind...

I feel 😟 😣 🙁 😮 😐 🙂 😃

What made you happy today? Draw or write.

Draw something beautiful.

Date:_____

Made in the USA
Coppell, TX
10 June 2021